Original title:
Shades of the Tropics

Copyright © 2025 Creative Arts Management OÜ
All rights reserved.

Author: Charles Whitfield
ISBN HARDBACK: 978-1-80581-610-2
ISBN PAPERBACK: 978-1-80581-137-4
ISBN EBOOK: 978-1-80581-610-2

Sun-Kissed Trails

Beneath the sun, the tourists dance,
With flip-flops squeaking, they take a chance.
Sipping coconuts with a silly grin,
How many times can they fall in?

Crabs scuttle past, with a keen eye,
As beach balls soar up to the sky.
Someone's hat flies, oh what a sight,
Chasing it down is pure delight!

Echoes of Exotic Blooms

In a garden bright, a bee lost its way,
Buzzing around like it's gone astray.
A lovely bloom knocks it off course,
As it fumbles about like a clumsy horse!

Laughter erupts at the colorful fuss,
While a butterfly joins, creating a buzz.
They twist and twirl in floral ballet,
Under a sun that's having its say!

Whirling Frangipani

Round and round go the dancers so spry,
A frangipani crown, oh my, oh my!
With each twirl, they lose a shoe,
Waltzing away like they're brand new!

The island tunes play tricks on their feet,
They hop, they skip, with fruity treat.
Pineapples drop from the trees like rain,
While laughter erupts, so wild, yet vain!

Tapestry of Twilight

As sunlight dips, the stars say, 'Hi!',
A parrot squawks, 'Oh, please don't cry!'
The fishermen cast their nets with cheer,
　Dreaming of fish — or maybe a beer!

A monkey swings down, steals a bite,
While losing its grip, oh what a sight!
It lands in a bucket, is that dessert?
With giggles erupting, who's feeling hurt?

Flourish of Flora

In gardens lush, where ferns play tag,
The daisies dance, with colors brag.
A parrot squawks, then steals a hat,
While sunflowers point, like chubby bats.

Bees buzz by, with clumsy grace,
Tickling blooms, a floral race.
The tulips wink, in sunny cheer,
As grasshoppers leap, give a loud cheer!

Luminescent Seas

At night the waves begin to glow,
Like disco lights, with a wild show.
A fish in shades of neon bright,
Wiggles past in sheer delight.

The crabs put on their cutest strut,
In tiny shoes, oh what a gut!
A porpoise jumps, does a twisty spin,
While seagulls cackle, 'Let's dive in!'

Dreaming in Bright Hues

A canvas wide, where artists play,
With paint and laughter, bright array.
The sun speaks gold, the sky's a tease,
As clouds wear shades of cotton breeze.

In every corner, colors blend,
A rainbow's party that won't end.
Each stroke a giggle, each splash a shout,
In this playful world, fun's the route!

The Rhythm of Rainfall

Pitter-patter on the ground,
Like tiny drummers all around.
The frogs rejoice, they sing a tune,
While puddles form a wobbly moon.

Umbrellas bloomed where folks had fun,
A dance of raindrops, everyone.
A slip, a slide, a cheerful yelp,
In this wet world, all joy is felt!

Resplendent Rainbows

In the sky, colors twist and twirl,
Each hue a joke, watch them swirl.
A red parrot cackles, in a feathered coat,
While green ones gossip, afloat on a boat.

Sunshine bounces, like a bouncy ball,
Catch the laughter, have a ball!
Flip-flops squeaking on the sandy ground,
Who knew joy could be this profound?

The Lure of Untamed Islands

Lost in laughter, on a hammock swing,
An iguana sings, 'Oh what a fling!'
Coconuts tumble, rolling with glee,
As a turtle jokes, 'Slow down, you see?'

Palm trees dance with a silly sway,
Inviting all to join the play.
The breeze whispers secrets, wild and free,
While beach crabs plot a grand jubilee!

Parrots in flight

Fluffy comedians up in the sky,
Cracking jokes as they flutter by.
'Polly wants a cracker!' one cheekily squawks,
While others just giggle, dodging the hawks.

Wings like rainbows, colors so bright,
In a comedy show, they take flight.
Their antics cause waves of laughter and cheer,
'Look at me!' they squawk, 'I have no fear!'

Harmonies of Habitat

In leafy jungles where the critters play,
The monkeys swing and shout, 'Hip, hooray!'
A toucan yells, 'Let's make some noise!'
While frogs join in with their ribbiting joys.

Caterpillars waltz beneath a bright sun,
Each little dance, just so much fun!
Chirping in rhythms, they sing out loud,
Creating a concert, drawing a crowd!

Whispers of the Parrot's Song

In the trees, the parrots squawk,
Like gossiping friends, they mock.
One says, "The mango's ripe today!"
The others argue, 'No way, no way!'

With beaks so bright, and tales so tall,
They laugh and mimic, they have a ball.
'Was it really you who stole that snack?'
'Not me! It was the green guy in the back!'

Coral Dreams Beneath the Sun

Fish in colors that glow and prance,
They're quite the actors, in a sea dance.
One clownfish wore a tiny hat,
While a turtle snoozed, oh how he sat!

Jellyfish float like balloons in air,
One tells jokes—who knew they could dare?
'I swear, I just saw a shrimp in socks!'
'No way,' says a fish, 'That's part of the stock!'

Emerald Canopies at Dusk

The monkeys swing, oh what a sight!
They drop their fruits, a funny fright.
One's wearing leaves, a stylish dress,
Says, 'I'm ready! Who'll be impressed?'

Lizards strut, like they're on stage,
In the fading light, they turn the page.
'Look at me! I can stick, I can crawl!'
'Oh please, no need to show off at all!'

Dancing Shadows on Golden Sands

Crabs have parties, throw feasts of shells,
While seagulls laugh at their sandy spells.
One crab moonwalks, the crowd goes wild,
While from a beach ball, a cat calls, 'Mild!'

A starfish posed for a beachy snap,
Said, 'I'm the star of this beach-map!'
The sunset giggles, wraps up the day,
The waves nod, 'What a show! Hooray!'

Blooming with Life

Bright flowers giggle in the breeze,
They dance and sway with playful ease.
Bees wear tiny hats, quite out of place,
While butterflies prance with a silly grace.

The sun dons shades, a cool little dude,
While fruits in baskets try to be crude.
A parrot squawks jokes, he's quite the show,
As lizards do limbo, moving real slow.

Lost in Verdant Vistas

In the jungle, the vines play tricks,
Swinging like monkeys, oh what a mix!
Frogs croak out tunes, quite out of tune,
While sloths take selfies under the moon.

Palm trees gossip in the hot, humid air,
While iguanas sunbathe without a care.
Scents of coconuts fill the whole place,
As toucans check hair with a mirror space.

Enchanted Bay

Seagulls wear crowns like royalty grand,
Sipping some piña coladas so planned.
Fish splash about with a wink and a flip,
While dolphins join in for a synchronized trip.

The sand tickles toes, what a fine feel,
As crabs do the cha-cha, that's their appeal.
Sunsets chuckle, painting the skies bright,
As starfish join hands for a magical night.

Cascades of Color

Waterfalls giggle, gurgling with glee,
While rainbows do cartwheels, so wild and free.
The rocks throw a party, all mossy and green,
Inviting the squirrels for the best scene.

Glowworms glow like little lamp lights,
While turtles hum tunes of old fishing nights.
Nature's a comedian, always on cue,
With antics so funny, they're too good to rue.

Emerald Waters

In a lagoon where ducks all wear hats,
Swim the fish that dance like acrobats.
Turtles throw parties, what a delight,
Splashing around, they party all night.

The sun's a spotlight, it shines so bright,
While crabs in the sand are a hilarious sight.
They wave their claws, pretending to clap,
For a show that makes everyone laugh!

The jellyfish jive, with style and flair,
While otters serenade, without a care.
Every ripple got laughter, oh what a scene,
In the emerald waters where joy reigns supreme.

Dance of the Hibiscus

Hibiscus blooms, oh, what a tease,
Waving their petals in the warm breeze.
They gossip of pollen, and brave bees in flight,
Chasing each other, oh what a sight!

They twirl and they swirl, in colors so bold,
Sharing their secrets, not one left untold.
With a wink to the orchids, they beckon them near,
"Come join our fiesta, there's nothing to fear!"

By sunset they sigh, as shadows creep near,
Sipping on nectar, plenty of cheer.
Petals look tipsy, from all of the fun,
Best dance in the garden, when day's almost done.

Secrets in the Breeze

The palm trees whisper, in gossip galore,
They swish and they sway, sharing tales of yore.
"Did you hear about Sandy? She lost her cool hat,
Now she's wearing a coconut! Fancy that!"

The breeze carries laughter, like music it flows,
Tickling the noses of sunburned toes.
A toucan's laughter, deep as the sea,
Echoes through canopies, wild and free.

Chatter from crickets adds to the jam,
As frogs pluck a banjo, oh look at the slam!
Fireflies join in, their lights dance in tune,
Secrets are dancing beneath the bright moon.

Coral Kissed Horizons

Beneath the sunset, corals giggle with glee,
As fish play bingo on the deep blue sea.
"Who'll win?" they ponder, all in good jest,
The lionfish yells, "I'm the very best!"

Seagulls dive down, trying to steal fries,
"Hey, don't be rude!" the crab grimly cries.
With a wink and a wave, he offers some shells,
"Come share my snacks; I hear they taste swell!"

The horizon blushes, a dramatic delight,
As the ocean chuckles, with stars coming bright.
Every laugh lingers, like foam on the shore,
In this coral kingdom, who could ask for more?

Sun-Drenched Tales

Sunbeams dance on banana peels,
A monkey slips, oh, how it squeals!
Coconuts drop with a thud,
While crabs break-dance in the mud.

Palm trees lean for a cool drink,
While toucans gossip, make you think.
A lizard struts with a silly gait,
In this sunny land, it's all first rate!

Fishermen sing with a splash and swim,
As they bicker over who's more trim.
Sandy toes and fishy smells,
Oh, what fun, under these shells!

Late-night laughs by the firelight,
A parrot joins in, squawking right.
In the tropics, joy's the game,
Every day is never the same!

Essence of the Tropics

Mangoes rolling down the street,
Sticky fingers, oh, what a treat!
Lizards giggle on a sunny rock,
Time for a dance, let's all flock!

Waves crash while surfboards glide,
A seagull steals snacks, can't let it slide.
Sun hats flop over big, loud grins,
And coconut drinks with silly fins!

The hammock sways, oh, what a swing,
While crabs march in a conga ring.
Each sunset paints a silly face,
In this tropical, fun-filled place!

Even the rain clouds seem to play,
As they splash around on a sunny day.
With every giggle, the good vibes swell,
In a paradise where all is well!

Hues of the Ocean's Embrace

Mermaids splash with a quirky flair,
As fishermen giggle and gasp in despair.
Octopus flips in a misfit dance,
While dolphins laugh—what a chance!

Flamingos strike poses, pink and proud,
While geckos perform for a cheering crowd.
Crabs in tuxedos stroll on the shore,
In this seaside soirée, who could ask for more?

The sun wears goofy sunglasses wide,
While turtles take their daily slide.
Sandcastles built with fashions galore,
Each one a palace, we can't ignore!

Oceans whisper secrets oh so near,
As waves tickle toes and bring forth cheer.
In this watery wonder, laughter's the key,
Join the fun, come splash with me!

Lullabies of the Lagoon

Crickets sing lullabies to the moon,
While frogs play banjos—a silly tune.
Fireflies waltz in glittering light,
As night wraps around with a giggling bite.

Alligators joined in a dance so rare,
A party of critters, without a care.
The stars twinkle like mischievous eyes,
In this magical realm, where laughter flies!

Bamboo shoots sway, keeping time,
As turtles drum on a shell with rhyme.
Laughter echoes through leaves so green,
In this lagoon, fun reigns supreme!

As dawn approaches with a yawn and stretch,
Giggling frogs tell tales, it's their best sketch.
With every ripple, joy is bestowed,
In this lagoon, life's a jolly road!

Swaying Palms

In the breeze, the palms take a bow,
Dancing wildly, who taught them how?
A coconut drops, with a comical thump,
The monkeys giggle, then all start to jump.

Beneath the sun, they sway with glee,
Shadows playing games, just wait and see!
A parrot squawks jokes, the crabs join the chat,
As the beach turns into a hilarious spat.

Each twist and turn, like a circus act,
Who knew palm trees could be so packed?
Fronds waving like hands, are they clapping too?
The island's a stage, with a laugh-out-loud view.

So join the fun, and grab your chair,
Listen to the laughter, floating through air.
With every gust, there's a story to tell,
In the jungle's embrace, laughter rings like a bell.

A Symphony of Color

Tropical blooms paint the scene,
Bright and bold, like a dream machine.
The hibiscus giggles, "Look at me shine!"
While the orchids whisper, "You're so divine!"

The sunflowers laugh, with their great big heads,
While daisies compete, in their white and reds.
A toucan strolls by, making faces galore,
His rainbow bill says, "Let's start a tour!"

Violets throw shade, they're feeling so cool,
While daisies and roses play it all fool.
"Pick me!" "No, me!" they all start to shout,
In the garden so vibrant, no room for doubt!

As colors collide in a joyful mess,
In this floral fiesta, who could guess?
The bees are the DJs, buzzing with cheer,
In this symphony of color, let's all just cheer!

Sunset Serenade

The sun dips down, with a wink so sly,
Painting the sky, as the birds fly by.
A flamingo trills, with a voice like a star,
"Don't forget your shades, it's a glowing bazaar!"

The ocean giggles, with waves frothy and bright,
Reflecting the glow, oh what a sight!
A crab does a dance, on the golden shore,
Spreading the news, "Hey, come dance some more!"

The clouds trampoline, puffing up high,
Casting funny shapes, as they float on by.
A dolphin jumps in, with a flip and a twist,
"Join my sunset party, you surely get missed!"

So grab your pals, and follow the song,
Dance with the tide, where we all belong.
As the sun waves goodbye, with a dazzling flair,
The world takes a bow, in this warm sunset care.

Whispering Mangroves

In the mangroves, secrets are shared,
Twists and turns, oh how they dared!
The mudskippers chuckle, their antics so sly,
As the fiddler crabs wave hello, oh my!

"Look at me dance!" says the sparkly prawn,
"Isn't this party just the best at dawn?"
The trees sway closely, holding big hands,
While they gossip about plans for island bands.

With roots like fingers, they tap out a beat,
In this swamp ballet, it's quite a feat.
Bats in the branches, they play catch the light,
While ghosts of the night prepare for their flight.

As the moon takes charge, with a silver grin,
The mangroves hum softly, let the fun begin!
In this jungle café, where the wild things meet,
The whispering winds bring laughter so sweet.

Sunlit Canopy

Beneath the palm, a squirrel's spree,
Chasing coconuts like they were free.
A toucan's shout, a playful tease,
As monkeys swing with such great ease.

In a hammock, I take a nap,
Dreaming of naps with a splash and a clap.
A leaf falls down—a gentle slide,
Now my drink has a leafy ride!

Swaying branches overhead,
Birds throw parties, no need for bread.
Banana peels thrown in the way,
Slip and slide, it's a fun-filled day!

The sun dips low, a golden cheer,
A party here, a dance right near.
With laughter ringing in the air,
Who needs worries when fun's so rare!

The Color of Coconut Dreams

Coconuts rolling down the beach,
With laughter ringing, they're out of reach.
Lime-green drinks in coconut shells,
Sipping sunshine, oh how it swells!

A crab in shades of pastel pink,
Pinching toes—don't stop to think!
Seagulls strut like they're on parade,
Making faces, they won't be swayed.

Sunbathers glowing like fried eggs,
Too much sun—oh, the legs!
A flip-flop war breaks out in style,
Chasing friends—they run a mile!

As night falls down like a velvet sheet,
Dancing shadows on the warm concrete.
With coconut dreams still up in the air,
We'll laugh and sway without a care!

Vibrant Echoes of Paradise

Echoes ring from a nearby shore,
With a hula dance, we just want more.
Laughter bounces off the palm fronds,
In this paradise, we're all correspondents.

A parrot squawks the gossip loud,
"Did you see that?" it calls to the crowd.
Sandy feet tap to the drumbeat,
Fun is a language we all can meet!

Juggling mangoes, oh the thrill,
Under that sun, we swallow our fill.
Surfboards crashing on the waves,
It's the silly dance of the coconut braves!

As moonlight sprinkles on the bay,
We laugh and dance the night away.
With colorful cocktails topped with fruit,
Who knew paradise could be so astute?

Lush Labyrinths

In jungles thick where vines do weave,
Lost my way, or so I believe.
But wait—is that a fruit I spy?
A snack while I contemplate my why!

Chameleons play hide and seek,
Thinking they're clever—oh, what a week!
Butterflies, too, in hues so bright,
Flap around with delight in flight.

A vine swings low—a perfect swing!
I grab on tight, it's a goofy fling!
"Look, I'm Tarzan!" I shout with glee,
But land in puddles—oh, oh, wee!

Trees whisper secrets with a breeze,
While laughing frogs throw down their keys.
In lush labyrinths, we find our way,
With jokes and laughter brightening the day!

Charms of the Canopy

In the jungle, a parrot sings,
Surrounded by all sorts of things.
Monkeys swing on vines with glee,
While sloths take naps on a tall palm tree.

Lizards dash with a splash of flair,
As toucans flaunt their bright, silly hair.
Each critter's a character, what a sight!
Nature's circus, pure delight!

Kaleidoscope of Flora

Petals dance with a colorful cheer,
Roses jealous of orchids near.
Vines whisper gossip, oh what a tale,
While daisies giggle, without fail.

Cacti poke fun at their leafy friends,
"Too much water? Your party ends!"
Ferns wave shyly, like it's a game,
In this garden, all seek fame!

Embrace of the Breeze

A gentle breeze steals your hat,
While butterflies laugh, "What of that?"
Dancing leaves, they swirl and twirl,
Even the flowers start to hurl!

Gusts play tricks with a loud whoosh,
As palm fronds sway in a silly swoosh.
"Hold on tight!" the breeze then teases,
In this wind, we're all such easy breezes!

Mirage of Mangroves

In waters shallow, crabs do prance,
Making a game of the water dance.
Fish peek out with a cheeky grin,
In this world, who knows where to begin?

Muddy roots tell tales of woe,
"Why are we here? Who knows, let's go!"
Snakes slide by with a wink and nod,
While otters play, not a care, what's odd!

Carved by Currents

A crab in a tuxedo, struts by the shore,
It pinches a shell, says, "What's this for?"
The waves giggle, tickling the sand,
While fish in bow ties dance in the band.

The jellyfish wiggle, quite out of place,
With an umbrella hat, they float in grace.
The dolphins laugh loud, they leap and twirl,
While a seaweed puppet gives it a whirl.

Clams play cards, and oysters deal,
With pearls as chips, it's quite the steal!
Each splash and giggle, a day full of fun,
In this party of critters, we've just begun.

So if you feel blue, or are lost in a wave,
Join the merry sea circus, it's sure to save!
From the playful tides to the ocean's great show,
Each ripple and laugh, let your worries go.

Fields of Fireflies

Glowbugs in dinner suits—what a sight!
They flash and they flicker, all through the night.
Strutting their stuff in a fancy parade,
While crickets compose tunes, serenading the glade.

The moon pokes its head, curious and wide,
Watching the dance floor where the critters reside.
A beetle in glasses reads the night news,
The latest buzz—green glow for a snooze!

Ants bring the snacks, tiny morsels and crumbs,
While ladybugs gossip about all the chums.
Each wink of a light is a laugh and a cheer,
In this glow-in-the-dark party, the fun's always near.

So grab your best bowtie and join in the song,
Dance with the fireflies, you can't go wrong.
Under the stars, find your groove and sway,
In this sparkly soirée, let the darkness play.

Luminescence of Leaves

The leaves do the cha-cha, a groovy delight,
Bouncing in rhythm, under the moonlight.
A squirrel sporting shades, takes the floor,
While branches do a limbo, begging for more.

Butterflies flutter like they've lost their map,
Twisting and turning, in a vivid clap.
The trees join the chorus, singing with glee,
As a hedgehog in sneakers discovers the spree.

Flashes of color in the midnight show,
As the fireflies join in, putting on a glow.
A raccoon in a top hat announces the fun,
This glowing leaf party's just begun!

So sway with the branches, twirl with the breeze,
In this funky forest, forget about ease.
Join the wild jam in your fanciest leaves,
Where even the moon chuckles and weaves!

Rhythms of Rainy Days

Raindrops are dancers, tap-tap on my pane,
Each puddle's a pool, oh what a terrain!
The frogs wear their galoshes, ready to sing,
While the thunder claps as a drummer in spring.

A snail with a shell that resembles a hat,
Slides down the sidewalk, oh, imagine that!
While ducks with umbrellas quack jazzy tunes,
And the rainbow joins in, a show of balloons.

The sidewalks become rivers, racing with speed,
As children splash joyfully, doing their deed.
The clouds toss confetti, a wet, wild parade,
In this rhythm of rain, fun's freshly made.

So let the rain fall, let the laughter cascade,
With dance in your heart, this party's well played.
Embrace the storm's giggle, let worries be swayed,
In the splash of each puddle, joy's serenade.

The Palette of a Hidden Cove

In a cove where colors clash,
A crab wears shades that make you laugh.
The fish all dance in polka dots,
While seagulls try to steal their spots.

The sunbeams splash on sandy toes,
While tourists ponder, 'What's that nose?'
A parrot shouts a wacky joke,
As coconut drinks spill with a choke.

Siesta time for lazy rays,
While beach balls roll in playful ways.
The local dogs in sunglasses chill,
Paw-prints leading to a thrill.

At twilight's end, the colors run,
And laughter echoes, oh what fun!
The palette hides yet sings so bright,
In this cove of quirky delight.

Echoes of Laughter Among the Palms

Among the palms, a giggle grows,
As monkeys trade their silly clothes.
A toucan crafts a makeshift hat,
While locals laugh and roll on that!

In the hammock, dreams collide,
A sloth gets tangled—what a ride!
Bananas fly, it's quite the show,
As sun-soaked breezes dance to and fro.

Each wave brings forth a chuckle tune,
A crab sings ballads 'neath the moon.
The rhythm of the night ignites,
With laughter soaring to new heights.

The palms sway gently, join the fun,
As friendly shadows laugh and run.
In this oasis of silly schemes,
Laughter mingles with our dreams.

Serenaded by the Soughing Wind

The wind whispers secrets in the trees,
While lizards dance with the greatest ease.
A breeze tickles every sunlit face,
As laughter sprinkles through this place.

On sandy shores, the tales unfold,
Of dolphins dressed in outfits bold.
With every wave, a chuckle grows,
As sea turtles strike up unique shows.

Seagulls squawk in humorous tones,
While beachside folk hum happy drones.
The stories spin like toppling kites,
And every heart is lifted to heights.

At dusk, the laughter wraps like a cloak,
In the stillness, we share the joke.
The wind, it sighs a giggling sound,
While the stars applaud from all around.

The Aroma of Tropic Skies

With scents that tickle every nose,
A garden's laughter brightly grows.
Papaya faces, smiling wide,
While playful mangoes try to hide.

The breeze brings panels of sweet delight,
As coconut jokes take flight each night.
A parrot spills the beans with glee,
On fruit salads and mischief spree.

Banana peels and laughter twine,
As hidden critters draw the line.
The air is fragrant, fun-filled schemes,
As jasmine weaves through sunny dreams.

Beneath the stars, sweet tales arise,
In the perfume of painted skies.
A vibrant feast for heart and mind,
In tropical whispers, joy we find.

Celestial Currents

In a hammock strung high, I swing to and fro,
While the sun paints the sky with a bright, fiery glow.
A parrot named Pete, full of mischief and zest,
Keeps stealing my snacks; oh, what a pest!

The waves crash below, with a splash and a roar,
As I sip on my drink and ask for some more.
A crab in a tuxedo struts by with a grin,
Says, "Life's just a dance, come join in the din!"

The stars wink at me, playful and spry,
While the moon tells a joke, oh my, oh my!
"A fish walks into a bar," it starts with a gleam,
"If it's such a good swimmer, why not join a team?"

But I laugh in the night, carefree and bright,
With nature as my friend, everything feels right.
So here's to the laughter that bubbles in glee,
In this funny little world, just you, crab, and me!

Fronds and Fantasies

Beneath a large frond, I take a big dive,
Where the lizards are plotting, and ants come alive.
A tortoise in shades, he's cool as can be,
Sips tea with a snail, they're chatting with glee.

The breeze starts to tickle, oh what a delight,
As I try to catch butterflies, all in my sight.
But they giggle and flutter, evading my grasp,
While a monkey with sass says, "You must try to clasp!"

A tree frog jumps high, aiming straight for my hat,
"Why wear it at all? Look, you're funnier flat!"
I chuckle and twirl, as I dance through the rain,
With creatures all joining, it's a wild refrain.

So let's sing to the quirks of this vibrant expanse,
Where every leaf quivers, and every bug prance.
With laughter a-twinkle, it's all quite the show,
In this forest of wonder, just let the joy flow!

Whispers of the Wild

The parakeets gossip in a colorful tune,
While squirrels in jackets hold a grand festoon.
"Why did the lion wear a hat?" asks a bee,
"Because he wanted to be the king of the spree!"

The flowers are giggling, the breeze swirling round,
As a hedgehog in boots rolls around on the ground.
A sloth in a hammock, so lazy and bold,
Sips cocoa with marshmallows, oh what a hold!

"Why run when you can lounge?!" declares a stout dog,
As a snail in a bowtie serves up some hot frog.
The deer stops to ponder, with a wink and a grin,
"Let's throw a big party; let the fun begin!"

So laughter erupts in the wild with great flair,
As creatures unite in a banquet to share.
In this carnival spirit, we dance and we sway,
Creating a ruckus; oh, what a display!

Twilit Tranquility

As dusk paints the sky with a splash of deep blue,
A penguin on skates whirls and glides through.
His umbrella's a twirl, catching stars in its seams,
While crickets perform their delightful night dreams.

The fireflies join in, flickering bright,
As frogs start their chorus, what a musical night!
An owl winks sagely from a branch high above,
Says, "Life's just a hoot; your heart is the glove!"

A cat with a monocle lounges with grace,
As he sips on his tea, wearing quite the face.
"Did you hear about the fish that swam to the moon?"
"Had a party with stars, left too soon for a tune!"

So let's tip our hats to the magic around,
Where laughter and whimsy in dusk can be found.
The night hums a melody, playful and sweet,
In this whimsical realm, life is an upbeat!

Cascading Colors

In the jungle, colors clash,
A parrot scoffs, 'Oh what a mash!'
Bananas wear a polka dot,
While pineapples sing, 'We're hot!'

The monkeys paint their tails so bright,
Swinging through trees, what a sight!
Mangoes tumble with a grin,
Saying, 'Join us, let's begin!'

A lizard in a tutu sways,
As limes giggle in a daze.
Coconut hats on heads so small,
A fruit party - come one, come all!

In this place of color spree,
Every hue laughs in glee.
A vibrant world, a painted dream,
Join the dance, feel the gleam!

Dancing Daisies of the Tropics

Daisies twirl on sunny days,
With shades of yellow, pink, and grays.
They whisper secrets, giggle loud,
In this meadow, they're so proud!

Bees wear tuxedos, buzzing tunes,
While breezes play on afternoons.
The daisies bow, they take a chance,
Inviting all to join their dance!

A worm does the worm with flair,
Spinning round without a care.
Wiggling grasshoppers jump to beat,
The daisies laugh, 'Oh what a treat!'

Sun sets low, they strike a pose,
As nighttime tickles, laughter grows.
The flowers dream of brighter days,
When joy blooms in all its ways!

Halos of the Twilight

Twilight whispers, stars appear,
Critters laugh without a fear.
Fireflies wear their little lights,
Dancing round in playful flights!

A chameleon goes out to dine,
He thinks a leaf looks just divine.
But as he sits, blooms start to tease,
'Oh, no more salad, please, oh please!'

The sloths hang low from twilight trees,
Throwing jokes like autumn leaves.
While crickets chirp a silly song,
The moon chuckles, 'You can't go wrong!'

As halos swirl in evening's cheer,
The night delights, the world draws near.
With laughter and light, the tales unfold,
A vibrant laugh in skies of gold!

The Canvas of a Caribbean Sky

Up high, a pigeon wears a hat,
It thinks it's suave, the silly brat.
Clouds laugh at its bold fashion flair,
While sunbeams tease like they just don't care.

The postcard sun's a joker too,
Painting rainbows for a bright debut.
Seagulls dance like they're on parade,
Chasing after the lemonade!

Palm trees wiggle in the breeze,
Dancing with grace, giving us a tease.
Birds chirp jokes, flying on a whim,
While the sunset hums a playful hymn.

In this land of mirth and delight,
The night brings stars, oh what a sight!
Moonbeams giggle as they drift by,
Painting smiles in the Caribbean sky.

Drifting on an Indigo Current

A fish in a tux, looking quite dapper,
Swims past a crab whose shell's a clapper.
Coral reefs giggle, colors collide,
As waves tell secrets beneath the tide.

A turtle's slow, but with flair he glides,
His shell a disco ball, he's got the vibes.
Pufferfish puff up just for the show,
Their bloated laughter helps the tide flow.

Jellyfish jiggle, bouncy and bold,
With laughable moves that never get old.
A manta ray flies high and free,
Squirting water, oh what glee!

In the depths where the sunbeams dance,
Creatures cavort in sheer happenstance.
The ocean sings a funny tune,
As fish throw a party 'neath the moon.

Vibrant Beats of the Caribbean Heart

A parrot croons a morning song,
While roosters join, they can't go wrong.
Coconut drums keep the sun on beat,
As the day sizzles under bare feet.

A limbo contest breaks the noon,
With a fellow doing a dance with a spoon.
The laughter echoes like coconut shells,
As he trips, oh how everyone yells!

Kids hit the waves, riding the tide,
Splashing and laughing, pure ocean pride.
The rhythm of life, it never quits,
Even crabs join in with their silly skits.

In a world full of music and cheer,
Where every day feels like a fairytale year.
The heart of the coast beats steady and strong,
In this vibrant land, we all belong.

Honeyed Light Through Coconut Palms

A squirrel swings, a nut in his grasp,
In search of treasure, but oh! What a gasp!
He tumbles down, but lands in soft sand,
With honeyed light, it's a glorious land!

Coconuts giggle, just hanging around,
Watching the antics that often astound.
A monkey drops in for a snack and a sip,
With honeyed watermelon, he's got a sweet trip!

The sun sets low, casting golden rays,
While fireflies dance in a playful gaze.
Each palm tree whispers a story of fun,
In a glow that warms everyone.

As night falls down, stars shoot their light,
Laughter mixes with crickets' delight.
A hammock sways under night's calm dome,
In this sweet haven, we're forever home.

Tropical Twilight

In the dusk, the parrots squawk,
While monkeys dance and the crabs gawk.
A lizard in a tiny hat,
Sipping juice—oh, how he's fat!

The sunset paints the sky with glee,
As palm trees shake a little spree.
A coconut drops, oh what a sound!
It bounces off the ground, so round!

A turtle in shades, cool on the sand,
Waving to all, like a rockstar band.
The fireflies flash like disco lights,
While the iguanas prepare for flights.

As night falls down with a goofy grin,
The crickets chirp of their midnight win.
With lights and laughs, the day is done,
In the tropics, oh what fun!

Footprints in the Sand

A crab scuttles past with quite a flair,
In his little shell, he thinks he's rare.
Footprints dance like a funny game,
While seagulls caw, 'Who's to blame?'

A beach ball rolls, oh where does it go?
Chasing the waves, putting on a show.
Umbrellas wave like they're in a race,
As children giggle, it's a wild place.

A flip-flop flings into the blue,
Right past a sunbather, who's feeling blue.
The jellyfish wobbles, such a delight,
Wishing on stars, still out of sight.

Even the sun wears a goofy grin,
As it sets, bidding the fun to begin.
Footprints fade, but laughter remains,
In the sand, where joy entertains!

Raindrops on Sunlit Petals

A parrot in rain boots, oh what a sight,
Dancing in puddles with pure delight.
Each raindrop bounces like ping-pong balls,
While flowers giggle and the petals call.

The sun peeks out, with a cheeky beam,
Sporting a smile, it's a sunny theme.
Dewdrops glisten on leaves like jewels,
Nature's jesters, playing with fools.

The frogs in the pond croak a sweet tune,
Sipping the rain while they bask under moon.
A butterfly slips; she lands with a plop,
The show never ends, this laughter won't stop.

And as the clouds play hide and seek,
The tropical land begins to speak.
With humor drizzled on every bloom,
It's a fun fest in nature's room!

Laughter of the Lagoon

A turtle swims with quite the flair,
Doing the backstroke without a care.
The fish all giggle, causing a splash,
As they wiggle and dance in a playful dash.

Water lilies clack like gossiping friends,
While the breeze whispers, 'The fun never ends!'
A frog leaps high on a lily pad throne,
Croaking his jokes in a wobbly tone.

The moon glows bright, a disco ball,
Reflections shimmer, they beckon all.
An otter slides down with a joyful cheer,
Making waves of laughter, everyone near.

In the lagoon's embrace, joy takes flight,
With giggles and bubbles that sparkle bright.
As night unfolds, the laughter remains,
In this tropical haven, fun reigns!

Celestial Rainforest

In the jungle's tight embrace,
Monkeys play a frantic race.
Parrots squawk with styles galore,
While sloths snooze and snore.

Lizards lurk on sunlit stones,
Dancing like they own the bones.
Chasing butterflies in a spree,
Who knew nature could be so free?

Vines dangle like a party hat,
As frogs leap from this and that.
Dining on some leafy treats,
While laughing at their own small feats.

So step inside this leafy scene,
Where life's a joke, and all's serene.
Each creature bears a quirky grin,
Oh, to be wild, where laughs begin!

Radiant Retreat

In a hideaway of vibrant green,
A dance-off where no one's mean.
Coconuts are drinks divine,
But watch out for that sneaky swine!

Parrots strut with bling so bright,
While iguanas join the fright.
Fruits fall down like nature's gift,
A picnic planned, oh what a lift!

Bees buzzing like they own the air,
While monkeys swing without a care.
Laughter bubbles through the trees,
Nature's party—bring the cheese!

So raise a toast to feathered friends,
In costumes loud that never ends.
This radiant retreat is a pandemonium,
Where every step is pure euphorium!

The Jungle's Palette

Colors burst from every scene,
With hues more vivid than you've seen.
Green like envy, red like fire,
Nature's brush—a wild choir!

Frogs in polka dots parade,
While toucans flaunt their finest grade.
Lizards with sparkles on their backs,
Dancing to the drumbeat's wax!

Each petal holds a silly tune,
Underneath the smiling moon.
Bees with shades of yellow glee,
Buzzing jokes as funny as can be.

Plantains swing in the breeze's dance,
As critters join in a funny prance.
The jungle's palette, bright and bold,
Where laughter's worth its weight in gold!

Azure Mirage

Underneath a sky so blue,
A parrot shouts, "What's new with you?"
With waves of laughter in the air,
Sandals lost? Who has a spare?

Crabs don sun hats, taking a stroll,
Building castles is their ultimate goal.
Fish grin with glittering flair,
As they play tag without a care.

Turtles giggle in their shells,
Making puns that surely sells.
Salty air with jokes afloat,
In this mirage, fun's the ultimate quote!

So watch for watermelons that roll,
They're the stars of the sandy shoal.
This azure mirage, a wild delight,
Where every day is pure delight!

Oasis of Dreams

In a hammock that's swaying, I dream of a pie,
With a coconut filling and a funny bye-bye.
There's a parrot who dances, makes me giggle and hop,
Claiming he's king of this tropical shop.

Palm trees are swaying, in rhythm they sway,
As I watch all the monkeys just planning to play.
They throw coconuts down with a laugh and a cheer,
Telling me jokes that only I hear.

The sun's casting shadows, so silly and bright,
While a crab does the conga under the moonlight.
A lizard appears, wearing sunglasses with flair,
He struts and he poses like he just doesn't care.

So come join the fun where the breezes are sweet,
With laughter and joy, there's no better retreat.
Leave your worries behind, let them drift away,
In this quirky paradise where silliness stays.

Coconut Crown

Oh, what a sight, in my crown made of kokonuts,
I strut down the beach, walking like I got guts.
The waves join the party, they splash and they crash,
As I dance like a fool, not caring to crash.

The crabs wear bowties, so slick and so neat,
They tap dance along, with their tiny little feet.
A fish wearing shades swims by with a grin,
I raise my coconut mug, let the fun begin!

The sun's like a spotlight, bright yellow and loud,
I serenade the dolphins, hoping they're proud.
But it's all in good fun, no worries in sight,
Just laughter and joy in this tropical light.

So grab your own crown and become a beach king,
Let the coconuts roll, let your laughter take wing.
For life's one big party with splashes and sounds,
Under the palm trees where the fun surrounds.

Melodies Above the Foliage

Can you hear them? The parrots sing high,
With voices so silly, they giggle and cry.
The tunes they are humming make the palm trees sway,
While the sun takes a bow, at the end of the day.

The critters all gather, for a concert so wild,
Bugs, frogs, and lizards, oh, each one a child!
They tap tap tap, on the leaves and the ground,
Creating the music that knows no bound.

A monkey on drums plays a beat that's sublime,
While iguanas strut, keeping perfect time.
Even the flowers dance with petals so bright,
Underneath the cool glow of the soft moonlight.

So let's join the chorus, with laughs that resound,
In this leafy theater, where joy knows no bounds.
For every green leaf should sway to this cheat,
In this funny concert where happiness meets.

Saffron Sunsets

By the water so smooth, the colors collide,
A saffron sunset, where laughter can't hide.
I watch as the flamingos do their best ballet,
On stilts made for giggles, they dance and sway.

Coconuts chuckle, bobbing each way,
As if they're just waiting for someone to play.
The colors are bouncing, so bright and absurd,
While I sit here pondering, with a musty old bird.

A monkey throws confetti, celebrating the night,
With a wink and a nod, he takes off in flight.
The crickets come out, with their buzz going strong,
Creating a chorus that just can't be wrong.

As the stars start to twinkle, they join in the fun,
In this laugh-fueled party, where all is well done.
So here's to the sunsets, that light up our days,
With colors and laughter in quirky displays.

Fruitful Abundance

Bananas slip, a monkey's gaffe,
Pineapple crowns in a juicy laugh.
Mangoes dance from the tall green tree,
As papaya plops, 'Oh dear, not me!'

Coconuts roll by, a bumpy race,
Guavas giggle, a tropical space.
Lemons throw jokes with a tangy twist,
While cherries wink, they can't be missed!

Eden's Embrace

In a world where berries bounce,
And sugarcane will sway and flounce.
Lime wedges shout, 'We're zest for fun!'
While coconuts play 'who's lost the sun?'

Fruits on trees wear smiles so wide,
Every peach is a cheeky guide.
A playful breeze gives them a wave,
While grapefruits joke, 'We're strong and brave!'

Tidal Tapestry

Oysters giggle at the shoreline's jive,
While crabs perform their silly dive.
Seashells gossip with a salty grin,
As starfish cheer, 'Let the fun begin!'

Waves tickle toes as the seaweed sways,
Dolphins laugh in bright, sunny bays.
An octopus juggles with all its strength,
'Come for a swim, enjoy the length!'

Spirits of the Coconut Grove

Under palm fronds, a party unfolds,
Coconuts shimmy, as laughter holds.
Tropical drinks with tiny umbrellas,
Fund the beach games, for playful fellas.

Parrots squawk out the latest news,
While iguanas join in on the snooze.
A fruit salad fight, oh what a sight,
With laughs ricocheting into the night!

Jungle Secrets Intertwined

In the jungle, vines do twist,
A monkey's dance, you can't resist.
They giggle and swing, oh what a sight,
As parrots squawk in morning light.

A sloth in pajamas, what a tease,
Sipping dew from the freshest leaves.
His eyelids droop, but don't you fret,
He's planning a party—don't you forget!

Creeping critters play hide and seek,
While snakes do laugh with a sly, cool sneak.
A tapir trips, mud on its snout,
Charmingly comical, without a doubt!

So join the fest, leave worries behind,
In this jungle, joy's all you'll find.
With laughter so loud, you can't contain,
Nature's jesters, on pleasure's train.

A Journey Through Luminescent Flora

In twilight's glow, the flowers bob,
With glow-worms dancing, doing their job.
A hibiscus red, with curls like hair,
Screams, "Let's party!" to the night air.

Lilly pads sail in a moonlit pool,
Toads croak their tunes, think they're so cool.
A museful breeze whispers silly puns,
While owls roll eyes at absent-minded runs.

From ferns that giggle to palms that sway,
The laughter blooms as the critters play.
Jumping jellies swirl in a vibrant show,
With every twirl, more joy to stow!

Join the ruckus, no frown allowed,
In this magical realm, be mirthful and loud.
With petals and laughter, they entwine,
In this dance of light, all things align.

Island Whispers

On sun-soaked shores, where coconuts grin,
Crabs throw a party with their tiny kin.
Surfboards wobble, then take a dive,
While the fish sing tunes that keep them alive.

Pineapples chime in with fruity flair,
A conch shell choir, beyond compare.
Seagulls cackle, with drama in flight,
While palm trees sway, basking in the light.

Vibrant sunsets, a canvas so sweet,
Dance-halls made of sand for dancing feet.
Each wave that crashes, giggles on creep,
While the ocean whispers secrets to keep.

So grab your hat, and join the fun,
The island's alive, it's just begun.
With laughter and music, we swish and sway,
In this tropical haven, let's laugh all day!

Tropical Reverie

In a hammock swing, dreams take flight,
With pillows of clouds, oh what a sight!
A sunset spills colors, a painter's delight,
As fireflies giggle, lighting the night.

The laughter of leaves, a giggling breeze,
Jellyfish pirouettes, with such ease.
Bananas juggle with playful zest,
As monkeys cheer in their leafy nest.

With sandcastle dreams that topple and sway,
The palm trees chuckle, come join the play.
While flamingos pose in the sunset glow,
Their one-legged stance steals the show!

A feast of smiles, all nature's jest,
In this reverie, we are truly blessed.
So dance like the tide, lift your heart high,
In this funny paradise, let's reach the sky!

Kaleidoscopic Shores

On the beach, my toes do dance,
In flip-flops that don't stand a chance.
The sun's bright rays make me look spry,
While seagulls steal my lunch awry.

Sandcastles lean like they're too tipsy,
While my sunscreen screams, "This is risky!"
I chase a crab, it darts and runs,
Laughing hard as I trip just for fun.

Beach balls roll like they have a mind,
While kids dive into waves, so unrefined.
The lifeguard snoozes, a sight so grim,
As I splash about - oh, how I swim!

The tide turns up with a gentle grin,
As sunburns shout, "You're doomed to win!"
With laughter loud, we'll chase the light,
Under palms where day meets night.

Chorus of the Dusk

As the sun dips low, the colors blend,
Laughter erupts, it's time to send.
Crickets chirp in a silly song,
While I skip along, where did I go wrong?

Bamboo sticks sway with a wobbly groove,
Coconuts roll and it's hard to move.
"Watch out!" I yell, but it's too late,
Falling like a star, all in good fate.

The fireflies twinkle, a light parade,
While my friends make jokes that never fade.
A dance of joy in this twilight gleam,
Where night becomes our sleepover dream.

Underneath stars that play hide and seek,
We roar with laughter, so wild and sleek.
Echoes of fun in the dusky air,
Join this chorus, if you dare!

Underneath the Tropical Skies

With piña colada dreams in hand,
I spy a parrot that can't quite stand.
"Polly wants a cracker," he caws with glee,
I chuckle as he steals my drink, oh, not me!

Palms sway gently in the warm breeze,
I attempt to juggle, they say, "Just freeze!"
A lizard joins in, with a wink and a glance,
Together we twirl, what a wild dance!

The sun's a jester, it tickles the sea,
While I chase my hat, what a sight to see!
My friend yells, "Catch it!"—I trip and I spill,
Watermelon juice gives my shirt a thrill.

Underneath skies, so blue and bright,
We laugh till late, it's pure delight.
With giggles echoing past the bay,
These moments of joy, we'll never betray.

Gilded Reflections

Mirror-like waters dance in the sun,
But my reflection? Say, "That can't be fun!"
I wave to the fish, they tease and they swirl,
While I trip on a rock and give it a whirl.

Bananas dangle, so bright and grand,
While I try my luck at a clumsy handstand.
The monkey chuckles, a cheeky delight,
As I tumble over—what a comedic sight!

The sun sets low, wearing golden hues,
While I'm stuck here with nothing to lose.
With laughter and bubbles, I lounge and play,
Time on this shore just slips away.

Reflections of joy in the light of the dawn,
As I finally accept I can't juggle at dawn.
But silly and happy, I'll claim the day,
In this paradise where we're free to sway!

A Dance in the Sunlight

Under bright skies, a pig in a hat,
Twirls with a parrot, how silly is that?
Coconuts giggle, the palm trees sway,
As monkeys join in to brighten the day.

Lizards wear glasses, quite dapper and neat,
While crabs hold a conga along the warm street.
With every salsa, they chuckle and cheer,
In the warmth of the sun, spreading laughter and cheer.

A toucan in flip-flops shouts, "Let's all play!"
Jumping on ponies to gallop away.
In this lively circus where colors collide,
The sun melts like butter while we all slide.

As the day ends, a sloth in a bow,
Sings karaoke while a flamingo plows.
With a wink and a wiggle, the crew bows in jest,
In the golden glow, they've truly been blessed.

Unfurling Petals of Paradise

Butterflies wearing polka-dot ties,
Flutter around with big, blinky eyes.
They sip on the nectar, sweet lemonade,
While singing loud anthems, unafraid.

Petals in tutus dance under the sun,
In this floral ballet, they're having such fun.
A bumblebee yodels, quite off-key,
As flowers all laugh in their colorful spree.

The daisies are gossiping, plotting a prank,
While roses in thongs form a gardeny rank.
At dusk they all gather, a party so grand,
With jams and sweet stories, it's perfectly planned.

With the moon's gentle glow, the fun just begins,
As the daisies break out in dancing spins.
In this petal-packed circus of whimsy and cheer,
Every bloom has a tale that we all need to hear.

Wandering Through Wild Oases

In the cool of the evening, a kangaroo hops,
Chasing a chameleon who makes funny stops.
With laughter like bubbles, they bounce through the night,

In this wild wonderland, everything feels right.

Turtles in shades strut under the stars,
On scooters with bears, leaving trails in their cars.
Palm trees chuckle, their leaves dance with glee,
While sand crabs groove like they're free from a spree.

A distant cowbell rings, sending out a call,
As hippos in bows host a water-ball.
With the moon shining bright, they jump in, they splash,
Turning the night into a vibrant bash.

As dawn starts to break, they sigh with delight,
In this oasis, everything feels just right.
With memories of laughter, fun tales to share,
They dream of the moments, a jubilant flair.

Surreal Celestial Gardens

Stars wear pajamas, zigzagging around,
Giggling as comets do tumbles abound.
In this cosmic ballet, the planets all spin,
With meteors having a tea party within.

Galaxies swirl in a colorful dance,
As aliens waltz with a tip and a glance.
With twinkling giggles and luminous hues,
Each constellation has its own funky shoes.

At dusk, the sun plays hide and seek,
While clouds in a frenzy cheekily peek.
With a wink and a joke, they blend day and night,
Creating a canvas of whimsy and light.

In this surreal garden where laughter ignites,
Each star has a story between day and night.
With joy in their hearts, they all swirl around,
In this cosmic playground where fun is unbound.

www.ingramcontent.com/pod-product-compliance
Lightning Source LLC
Chambersburg PA
CBHW072120070526
44585CB00016B/1512